A NEW WAY TO LIVE

Humanity's Opportunity in a Post COVID-19 World

CHRIS FORMAN

TABLE OF CONTENTS

INTRODUCTION

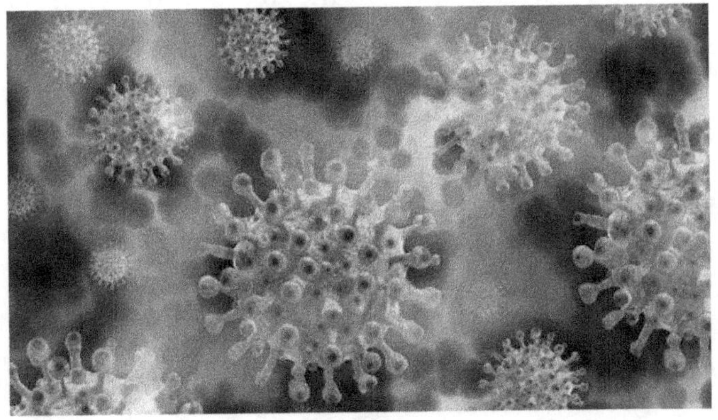

I'm writing these ideas while the world is in the midst of the COVID-19 pandemic. Most people have been self-isolating or practicing social distancing for about three or four weeks now. It has become overwhelmingly obvious and apparent that humanity must change its ways and find a new approach to living. It's time to create a better relationship with the earth—a newfound connection to the place that sustains us and nourishes our body and soul.

This is our wake-up call to action…our moment to realize that we can no longer continue to treat each other and the planet with disrespect and carelessness. We truly are at a crossroads. Will we finally become aware of how interconnected everything really is, or will we remain asleep to the clear-cut choices that we now must make? These are decisions that will determine our fate—a wiser and more enlightened way of life for our future is at stake. If we believe in kindness and the power of love, we just may make it out of this challenge with a brand-new state of BEING!

I would like to propose some optimistic suggestions on how we can best aspire to a more evolved state of awareness. A set of principles and values that can lift us all up to a higher level of relating to each other and to this planet that we call home.

This can be our breakthrough moment—our opportunity to turn this crisis into a positive transformation for all of humanity.

What do you say?

Are you prepared and excited about
this new possibility?

Are you truly ready for a more powerful and
rewarding approach to living and loving in
the twenty-first century?

CHAPTER 1

UNITY

Where to begin? What's the first step? How about the profound realization that everything in this world is connected?

The earth and all that's in it is really one big interrelated web of life. One ripple in this vast ocean of *being* can be felt throughout its entirety. The coronavirus has made this abundantly clear. We can no longer live with an "us vs. them" mentality. The truth is that this existence is now all about WE—as in, "We are all in this together." We have to get our shit prioritized, and we can discover a much more unified way of loving one another and the planet. This is our chance to come out of this coronavirus challenge with a deeper sense of connection and a newfound understanding of a wiser way to BE.

There is strength in numbers, and the more people we can get to awaken to this new reality, the more we can ensure that our future is bright and inviting. When the light comes on inside the collective consciousness, we will find our path to a much better tomorrow. All it will require is an open heart and a willingness to grow and become the united family that has always been our destiny. This is our time to shine—our next step in the evolution of mankind. We can most definitely do this, and a shift in our perspective will take us to places we can only imagine. Let's continue on and always try to remember that we're all in this together—one humanity, one world and one complete expression of love.

All the great mystics in history share a common experience in achieving heightened states of awareness and being. They have all felt the incredible oneness and connection to everything that exists. They have witnessed the walls of separation melt away and realized that ultimately there is no true duality in the universe. It's a euphoric and mind-blowing understanding that all matter, all energy, all consciousness, is really just one great cosmic entity.

I personally have yet to experience this higher state of oneness, but some brief glimpses of this plane of being have been unveiled to me at various points in my life. I think it's what they call being "in the zone" or being in a state of "flow," where you are so completely in tune with your surroundings that you absolutely lose sight of any distinction between you and the outside world. It's like you're part of a much bigger reality, and you feel there is <u>no</u> separation from this grander notion.

Any sense of disconnect has disappeared, and there's an overwhelming feeling of bliss as you join this magnificent dance with connection. No thought is required in this experience. All you simply have to do is let go and surrender to the higher wisdom that knows exactly all the right moves. The yogis and the gurus of this earth have all been privy to this amazing way of being; but this awareness is not limited to just sooth seekers. We all possess the ability to reach across the divide and connect to a singular state of mind.

Can you imagine what the world would be like if more and more of us were able to attain this profound level of existence? Can you visualize the awesomeness of a planet where its most sentient creatures have finally opened their eyes and minds to a completely enlightened way of living? I believe this will be our next giant step in the evolution of humanity's never-ending path to unfoldment and fulfillment. We are on the verge of a huge step forward and a new magical carpet ride to love and happiness.

CHAPTER 2

THE WISDOM OF SHARING

As things unfold in the new reality of the pandemic, we are realizing how essential it is to share with each other. The cry out for the need for protective masks, gowns, ventilators and hand sanitizer has mobilized people to reach out and give whatever medical supplies they can spare to the places that are having the biggest challenges. Big companies, small businesses and even private individuals are uniting in an effort to provide essential goods and services to those that require them.

We're awakening to the power of generosity and compassion and to that old expression that's always been a part of human history: "Where there's a will, there's a way." We're discovering the magnitude and magnificence of the willingness to come to the aid of others and that if we all join together in a common purpose, the strength of our collective souls knows no bounds.

We see this through the many examples of the heroes of this moment in time. People who are giving food to those who are hungry, those who are providing services for others free of charge, companies and landlords who are foregoing debts and rent that is due. We're beginning to understand that there is incredible gratification in looking after one another, and if we <u>all</u> pitch in, there's practically nothing we can't accomplish. There is tremendous satisfaction in sharing what you have to offer and this may just be the perfect opportunity to give the world whatever special talents or sentiments you possess.

Imagine if this new situation we now live in could snowball into an expanding movement…a desire to freely provide our global family with the abundance that only some of us have been able to enjoy. If we all decided to jump in and do our part, the world could be utterly transformed and become a home that we all thrive in and are proud of.

Is it really that simple? Is it really that easy? Is it even possible? Absolutely! We're seeing it all over. We're doing it right now! Even though it's taken a planetary crisis to get our attention, it doesn't take away from the fact that we already know how to do this. All that's required now is an awakened desire to make it happen. If we deeply feel and know that a higher level of generosity and sharing is possible, we can change the earth forever and give our species a profound new way of being and a fresh new lease on life.

Have you ever heard that old expression "it's better to give than to receive"? Do you think that's true? Is life more satisfying and rewarding when we share what we have? Are we open to the idea that if we freely offer what we can to others, it will come back to us in plentitude?

I can only speak to my own experiences in life. This much I do know—whenever I have let life's riches and blessings flow through me and shared them with the world, I always felt a great sense of gratification and love. Being generous with your human family can light up your soul and deeply enrich your heart. Ever since I was a little kid, I enjoyed giving away what I had. Connecting to the idea of abundance and passing that along to whoever you choose can spread an immense wave of fulfillment. The feeling can be contagious—the more we do it, the more everyone comes out a winner!

Whenever I win something, or I receive a gift, or I possess more than I require, I instinctively share it with whoever is around me. It's an awesome experience to see someone's face break into a smile when they are given an offering of generosity. Most people will inevitably do the same for the next guy.

Once you get this ball rolling, there's no way to stop it if everybody's on board.

Throughout my life, I have been privileged enough to have a multitude of gifts showered upon me. What better way to relish everything that the universe has provided than by freely letting it glide through your hands and into the arms of another. It can be whatever your spirit desires—from something as simple as home-baked bread to an extravagant treasure that means a great deal to you, but one that you know will be savored even more by the one who is receiving it.

Imagine if we ALL did this…freely offering whatever we can to anyone who is open to the flow of reciprocity. Wow, what an amazing world it would be—a planet filled with unlimited hope and love. A life filled to the brim with goodies for everyone. This is the future that awaits us. Get ready for it!

CHAPTER 3

A TIME FOR HONESTY

If we really plan on pursuing a new way of living, then it is absolutely essential that we always seek the truth. Creating a better path forward will require us to take a long look in the mirror and be honest with ourselves.

Being truthful takes great courage and humility and opens us up to all the scars and wounds that we've experienced on this road to recovery and renewal. If we are serious about coming out of this crisis with an elevated sense of purpose, then we're going to have to stop and stare at where we are really at.

We've been dozing at the wheel for a long time now and are getting a taste of cold, hard reality. Let's be honest. Do we really think that everything is going to go back to the way it was before? Do we even want it to?

Some of the best medicine is the bitter kind. We have been pushed into a corner. Now it's up to all of us to dig down deep and be willing to step into a place we've never known before. At times, we have been self-absorbed, careless, ignorant and foolish. We've taken many things in life for granted. Now that they've been pulled away from us, we're feeling anxious and afraid. Being real with ourselves isn't easy, but it's necessary if we're going to achieve the growth and results that we are looking for.

One day, when I was 11 years old, I was riding my bicycle with my friends. We were peddling and moving very fast, tying to outpace each other. All of a sudden, I hit a patch of loose gravel, and my front tire abruptly turned forcing my handlebars to swing wildly to the left. The front wheel dug into the stones, and I went flying into the air. Unfortunately —and painfully—I landed directly on my face, and my mouth hit the road with a sudden crunch. I immediately felt the crack of my two front teeth as they connected with the concrete. My mouth instantly began to burn, and there was blood gushing out of my top lip.

I think in that moment I was in shock and didn't realize how bad it really was until I got home and looked at myself in the bathroom mirror. Believe it when I say, it was *grotesque*! I could hardly even accept what was staring back at me; there was cold hard truth right in front of my eyes. I had broken two of my permanent front teeth, and they were going to have to be pulled. (I had already lost my baby ones.) You talk about a freaking gut-punch—I was slapped around and confused. What the heck was happening to me? What was the future going to look like?

This is how many of us are feeling right now with the pandemic upending our world. We are stunned and disoriented; we're dazed and afraid. A lot of people are wondering what is coming in the days ahead, and what is going to happen to the planet. And just like I had to deal with the discomfort and suffering that goes with getting my teeth knocked out, we're going to have to cope with having our lives smacked around.

The brutal truth is that life is never going to be the same again. But this doesn't have to be a frightening or a hopeless situation. Just like I picked myself up off the bloody road and faced my new reality, we can be honest and courageous with our current predicament. We can brush ourselves off, clean up our scrapes and bruises and make a commitment to move forward with our lives.

We have the ability to see our battered reflection and still decide to live our lives with a better understanding of what it takes to come out on top. Time will heal most wounds. We just have to believe in ourselves and be honest and open with each other. We can always get new teeth, and we can always design an improved and exciting new way of living.

Whenever I am working behind the wood in my job as a bartender, I commonly greet customers with a friendly "How are you?" or "How's it going today?" Of course, there are many different responses. One that stands out in my mind is when a customer answers back with some variation of, "Well, I'm still alive…every day above ground is a good day."

Typically this type of comment comes from an elderly gentleman. Most bartenders just smile and nod their heads in agreement. However, I am *not* your typical bartender. When I hear this statement, I *always* reply back with something like, "Oh? That's great! So tell me…*why* do you feel this way?"

I genuinely want to know the <u>reason</u> why they are happy to still be here. Why are they pleased to be alive?

The answers I received to these inquiries reveal an incredible understanding of what's really significant to the particular person. Whatever they say to me tells me so much about who they are, and what they value. They may say that they're grateful to be living because they get to see their grandkids. Or maybe they are looking forward to an upcoming event or special occasion. Some may come back with something as simple as they're just content in being able to enjoy a good beer and a chat with a friend. Whatever the reason is, I always find that just having the exchange brings the person closer, and I sense it makes them feel heard and understood.

The questions I ask really are crucial questions for all of us to ask ourselves.

"Why can I be happy to be living and breathing today?"

"Why am I thankful for the gift of simply being here?"

Contemplating these questions can lead us to immense truth. Everyone, no matter their age, can benefit from pondering these questions. The questions lead us to clarity and purpose, and can spark a rush of gratitude and appreciation. If you take the questions seriously, they offer a profound opportunity to get in touch with your inner self and a powerful reminder of why you are really here.

Being honest and open with yourself and with others is tremendously rewarding and can deeply enrich your life if you make a habit of it.

So, if you ever get the chance to ask someone why they are grateful to be alive, go for it. I promise you it will be an interesting interaction, and you just might find out more than you could ever imagine.

CHAPTER 4

THE POWER & PLEASURE OF NATURE & TECHNOLOGY

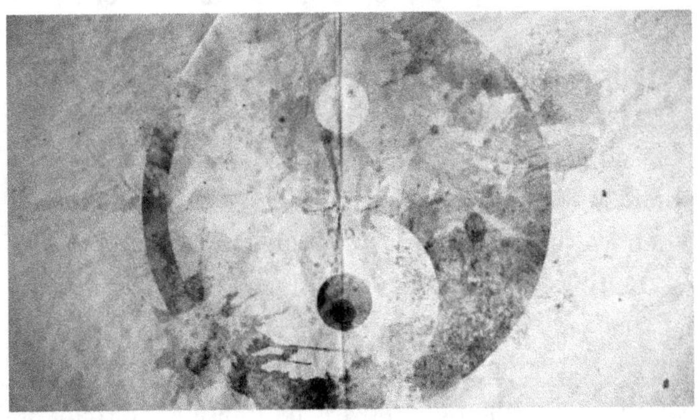

Now that many of us are spending so much time in our homes, we are relying on our devices even more to keep us connected. Social media is allowing us to communicate with each other from the safety and comfort of our living rooms. Staying in touch with those we love and care about is essential during these uncertain times, and it's extremely important for our mental/emotional health that we are able to share our feelings with those we are closest to. We are *most definitely* social creatures who thrive when we get the right amount of attention and interaction with our fellow human beings.

However, we are also still part of the natural world, and it's just as necessary (if not more) that we stay in sync with the physical environment. We are living, breathing, sentient animals that require clean air, fresh water and proper nutrition. Awareness of our reliance on the natural environment for substance and survival is imperative.

The virus emerged from the physical world, and our susceptibility to its advances has made it abundantly clear that the solution will be uncovered when we can find the right balance between living within these two spheres of influence.

Our advances in science and technology have been astounding, and the accelerated pace of change has increased the demand for us to adjust and adapt. Now is the critical moment when we will be required to create a new relationship with both our technical prowess and our undeniable dependence on the earth's life-sustaining abilities. This is one of the biggest challenges facing humanity—how do we find the right mix of scientific ingenuity and old school connection to our natural home? How do we discover the ideal recipe for success?

I am going to use my wife's ongoing challenge with cancer to illustrate one possible way we can find the perfect combination of the two sources of strength. My wife Nicole has multiple kinds of cancer. Her two biggest challenges are multiple myeloma (bone marrow cancer) and melanoma (skin cancer).

Nicole has contended with these unwelcome guests for years now and has shown great courage throughout all of her treatments and procedures. I'm continually amazed at how she has discovered just the right way of using both medical technology and the therapy of the natural world to heal her body. Her willingness to listen to her oncologist's recommendations, while at the same time paying attention to her instincts, has proven invaluable.

Nicole knows that there is powerful wisdom in balancing both scientific knowledge and her own intuition. She understands that breathing in clean, fresh air; drinking cool, clean water; and eating healthy, nutritious food is just as important as taking her prescriptions. She realizes that an invigorating walk through our local park is just as significant and beneficial as the treatments in the hospital. She has found her happy medium, and it's the reason why she is still alive. It's a true blessing, and the two of us are so grateful–a potent and powerful mixture of two great forces; the yin and yang of science and spirit.

A similar balance will also provide our answer to the COVID-19 situation and serve as a guiding light to all the new challenges that will come our way in the future.

CHAPTER 5

A BRAVE NEW WORLD

I just finished reading Aldous Huxley's *Brave New World*. While written in 1931, it offers much to consider in thinking about the society we will build as we emerge from the lockdown. The talking heads in the media and everyday people alike predict that our civilization will be changed forever because of this pandemic. I truly hope they are right. I'm not looking at this possible alternative future as a diminished or pale representation of our old ways. I envision an awakened earth, an expanded sense of awareness and intention…a better balance between human ingenuity and the ancient wisdom of the natural world.

Huxley imagines a future marked by a struggle between the traditions of the past and the modern, comfortable creations of contemporary society. There's conflict involving the desires and passions of the savage Homo sapiens and the more "evolved" preferences and conditioning of the brave new species that has been purposely designed by the *powers that be* in the not-too-distant-future.

I predict a dynamic like Huxley suggests will play out for us as we decide how we intend to live in the post-pandemic world.

Do we want to live and breathe in a reality where we've chosen to reconnect with the earth and respect its wishes to co-exist in a harmonious, symbiotic relationship?

Or, are we going to push forward with an increasingly disturbed and haphazard approach that disregards the natural rhythms of life and relies instead on even more technological solutions that may ultimately upend our collective apple cart?

Clearly some things have gone haywire for us. The next few years are going to determine if we will use this unique opportunity to take our progression in a whole new direction. This is our chance to shift our perspective and place a newfound emphasis on the health and wellness of the earth's ecosystems and our own spiritual well-being. This is our moment to merge the incredible intelligence of the human mind with the infinite possibilities of Cosmic Consciousness. Let's roll up our sleeves, get our hands dirty and find a deeply satisfying combination of the human will and the forces of Mother Nature.

How about we use our amazing inventions and tools for the betterment of mankind, instead of as distractions and ways to "kill time?" Spending hour upon hour looking at social media and seeking validation from others is not going to support us in our quest to realize the vision we desire. If we open our eyes and hearts to the questions that Aldous Huxley proposed, we can finally realize that the answers lie within the balance found between our inevitable evolution and that of this incredible blue marble we call home.

CHAPTER 6

COOPERATION: MUTUAL RESPECT & UNDERSTANDING

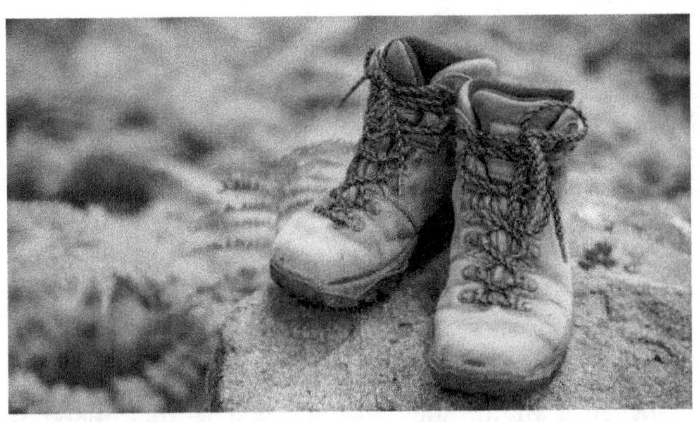

Now in order for us to move forward with a better approach to living, it's essential that we do so cooperatively. There are a lot of different opinions out there about what's best for humanity and the planet, and it's crucial that we take on this endeavor with a conscious intent to be respectful of other points of view. No one has a monopoly on **all** the answers. It benefits everyone if we always try to be considerate of a variety of perspectives. Ensuring success requires understanding the big picture and getting as many people as possible on the same wavelength. This won't be easy, but it's imperative because the more everyone feels they've been heard and their points of view have been taken into consideration, the more effective we will be in getting everyone on board. This is going to be a collective effort, so the more souls we can get aligned, the better our chances of achieving a positive outcome.

My wife and I got married in Key West back in 2011. The wedding we planned was a huge success and one of the best days of our lives. The location was gorgeous, the food was fantastic, the drinks were flowing and the music and dancing were everything we'd dreamed of. We even had drag queens crash the party—on purpose! It truly was a day of celebration and love.

Now the reason this event was such a perfect day is because of all the amazing people that made it happen. Our wedding planner had some great ideas, and his execution of all the details was a marvel to behold. The caterers, the DJ, the florist, the trolley driver, the guests...everyone played their part with such a willing spirit. We couldn't have asked for anything more. There were so many awesome moments and it was because of the loving, cooperative behavior of all the participants. When people enter into a commitment with an understanding that everyone's participation is valued and respected, there is an unmistakable feeling of harmony. The sum really is greater than the parts. This is a powerful concept to remember and put into action.

If we are serious about coming out of this pandemic with the strong desire for change and a renewed vision for the planet, we are going to have to make sure that we do it *together*…with as much teamwork and loving participation as possible. We are on the cusp of something big. The more we can get people united, the better chance we will have of creating an enlightened future.

One of the things I've been doing during the lockdown is watching the evening news. I flip between three different channels every night: CNN, Fox News and the CBC. Now the reason for this is because it gives me a better perspective than just watching one channel only. The various points of view on the pandemic are interesting, surprising and sometimes a little frightening. There are times where you can't believe they're actually reporting on the same story. The chasm between the outlooks can be quite shocking, and it makes me wonder if we are living on the same planet. I believe it's always beneficial, however, to get a variety of opinions and observations on a myriad of topics as it gives a wide range of options to pick from or from which to form your understanding.

If someone is simply looking at one program only (which many people do), then they are missing out on other possibilities that may change or enhance their perspective. When we can see the world through another's eyes, it gives us the opportunity to empathize and more fully comprehend what is *actually* happening.

The truth is that everyone has their own agenda, their own reasons and their own vantage point. Walking in another's shoes and contemplating their path can expand our awareness and give us a much better sense of why people do what they do.

It isn't always easy to make this choice, but it's crucial that we do so if we honestly desire to move forward with life in a more progressive and evolved approach. We may not agree with someone else's proposed solutions, but at least we have an idea of what they are thinking and feeling.

The world is a diverse, complex and at times complicated creature. All we can do is try our best to figure out a loving path to a mutually successful outcome. So whatever source of information provides you with your daily cup of news, it's essential to remember it is only *one* out of many sources and perspectives. It's up to each of us to slip on someone else's boots and feel what it's like to take a walk on a different road.

CHAPTER 7

HONOR YOUR BODY

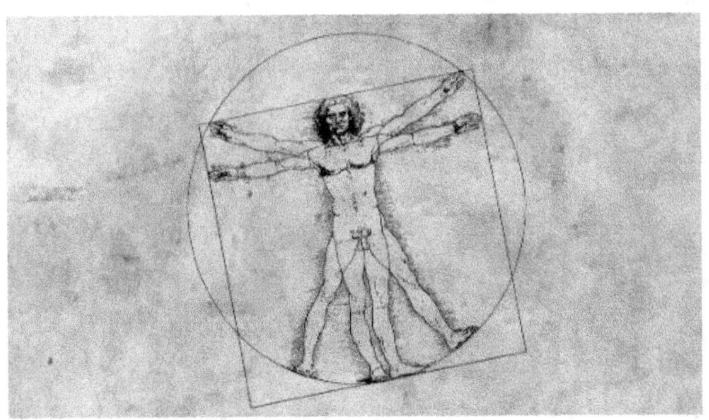

There's an ongoing debate during this pandemic as to <u>why</u> people of color are disproportionately suffering from the virus. Those who live in low-income neighborhoods and places of high-density housing are much more likely to feel the effects of COVID-19.

Many of us are asking *why?* Why is this hitting certain areas harder than other locations?

Well…as seems to be the case in life—it's a complicated story. There isn't always an easy explanation for how or why certain situations arise.

One thing we know for sure is that if you are already struggling with wellness issues or living a lifestyle that is laced with unhealthy choices, your vulnerability to a viral outbreak like this one are potentially increased.

We all are aware to varying degrees of the value and importance of taking care of our bodies. Our physical vitality is essential in ensuring that any microbiological threats are taken care of. The human immune system is constantly on the lookout for outside invaders. It's important that we do our best to make sure our bodies are strong and prepared for possible challenges.

My time as a bartender has given me the privilege of being intimately involved in the lives of many a patron. I vividly remember a regular customer of mine who was suffering from a reoccurring sore throat. He ended up going to the doctor and was eventually diagnosed with cancer in his larynx. He was told that if it was left untreated that his chances of survival were pretty slim. He was faced with the prospect of either losing his life <u>or</u> dealing with a treatment plan that would probably result in a permanent loss in his ability to speak. This is a choice that no one would ever want to make.

Surprisingly enough, he decided that there was a third option—an idea that was suggested to him by some of his close friends. He chose to change his diet and to self-medicate with cannabis. He nourished his body with protein, vegetables and cool, clean water. He eliminated most of his sugar intake and kept physically active. He consumed marijuana on a daily basis and did everything he could to give his physical temple the best chance of defeating the cancer.

Now, what do you think ended up happening? Was there a happy ending? You better believe it! Not only did his tumor disappear from his throat, but he also ended up feeling healthier and stronger, and he felt he had a whole new lease on life. People were amazed at his success story, and they noticed that he was so much more at peace and could sense his immense gratitude for being alive.

This wonderful real-life result can be a lesson to us all. If we open our eyes to the magnificence of the human body and take good care of this amazing vehicle we've been given, we can not only rise above the challenges of a virus, we can also reap the fantastic rewards of feeling zestful and full of life.

We all inherently know that our anatomies are a gift, and this one and only present should be cherished and respected. Our collective efforts will triumph over COVID-19, and hopefully we will realize just how significant it is for us to love and honor our bodies and make sure we stay awake to this newfound understanding.

CHAPTER 8

THE BODY TEMPLE

This is me…slim, happy, confident and <u>free</u>. I like how I look and enjoy how I feel. I can go to the beach if I want to, wear whatever clothes I prefer, and know that I am blessed with a wife who thinks I'm sexy and handsome. However, this wasn't always the case for me. At one time, my relationship with my body seemed much different than today.

Have you ever been teased? Have you ever been made fun of? Have you ever felt you were unusual and inadequate?

I know how it feels. It's hurtful and embarrassing. It seems so painful and unfair. When I was a kid, I was always really skinny. It didn't matter how much I ate or how much I exercised; I was just naturally a slim, lean guy. My arms and legs were thin, and my Adam's apple stuck out too far. Choosing pants could be agonizing for me because I had no butt at the time. Usually they wouldn't fit right, and I would struggle to keep them from falling down too low. I always thought corduroy pants looked best on me. Remember corduroys? I never even wore a pair of blue jeans until I was 18 years old because I was afraid I wouldn't look right in them.

It seems so silly now, but man did it feel real at the time. So, what changed for me? Why do I feel blessed today to have the slender frame that at one point in my life I was ashamed to inhabit?

I think it happened when I went away to university and moved to a much bigger city. I was suddenly surrounded by people of diverse colors and styles, including all sorts of body shapes and fashion choices. Some of the people genuinely didn't seem to care at all about what anyone else thought of them.

It was exhilarating! It was beautiful! It was liberating!

I became aware that it was healthy to love your own distinct look and that being unique is something to celebrate. I awoke to the beauty of my own contours and knew that, in my own way, I was wholly splendid. I fell back in love with myself when I realized how fortunate I was to be healthy and strong and that I was perfectly okay just the way I was built.

Our unique differences make life interesting. I truly hope that anyone who has ever felt awkward, self-conscious or afraid about their body image or appearance really gets this concept. We are all wonderful in our own particular way and loving ourselves and our bodies is one of the greatest gifts we could ever give or receive.

CHAPTER 9

RESPECT THE EARTH

Just as it is essential to take care of our physical bodies, it's also just as important to nurture and respect our physical home—the earth itself. Whether we realize it or not, our planet is a living, breathing entity that we <u>all</u> depend on for our very existence. We are utterly reliant on the earth's natural systems to ensure our physical survival: pure, fresh air; cool, clean water; and tasty, healthy food are what this globe provides us. We're finally waking up to the truth that so many aboriginal peoples have been telling us for centuries; the first nations of this world have always been aware of the critical connection we share with Mother Earth. They have respect for this beautiful life-sustaining planet and have built their customs and culture so as to honor this cherished relationship.

We are profoundly affected by our natural home's influence on our daily lives.

What is one of the first things that most people do every single day when they wake up? They check to see what the weather is like outside. That first peek out the window in the morning can determine how we feel about how our day is going to be. Is it sunny out, or is it cloudy? Is it warm, or is it cold? Is it windy, or is it calm outside? Our mood and disposition are directly related to the prevailing climate we sense when we first greet the day.

As I write this chapter, we have now been in lockdown for around five weeks. Interestingly enough, I have read in the newspaper and seen on television that we are noticing the natural world is already changing. The air seems fresher; the lakes and rivers look cleaner; we're seeing animal behavior that is different—including wild goats roaming into some small towns. It's like we're allowing the earth to finally catch its breath and we've temporarily stopped the full-scale bombardment of smoke, chemicals and pollution. In less than forty days—we're observing that the sky looks bluer and dolphins are appearing in new places. We can actually hear the sounds of songbirds and even the wind rustling through the trees in urban areas.

We are being allowed to reconnect with the rhythms of the natural world like never before. I find myself having sensations and feelings that I haven't had since I was a boy in southern Ontario.

When I was a kid, I spent countless hours and days exploring the lake, rivers, meadows, cliffs and beaches that I was so fortunate to live near. I experienced thunderstorms, bird migrations, insect invasions, blizzards, wild berries, crab apples and water funnels. It was a natural wonderland.

My friend and I used to build forts in the Carolinian forests that thrived all around us. We immersed ourselves in the sensory pleasures that being in the wild could provide. We swung from vines that hung from the treetops; we collected fireflies and caterpillars; we got dirt under our fingernails and pickers in our socks; we tasted the flowers of wild clover and wrestled in the foliage that carpeted the hillsides of the lake.

The smells of the natural world are unmistakable —lilac bushes, apple blossoms, fallen leaves, rain, or how about the scent of a driftwood campfire? We had no idea at the time how the environment was seeping into our souls and how deeply connected we were to its magical embrace. It's only now that I am a little older and wiser that I can truly appreciate how absolutely amazing the outdoors really is. It's in our DNA; it's in the stardust; it's our very essence. It's an intimate connection that nourishes our very being and a blessing that can sustain us throughout our entire lives.

Have you ever seen the video series *Planet Earth*? It's a collection of shows narrated by a man named David Attenborough. The series showcases the magnificence and incredible biodiversity of the natural world. From the awesomeness of the oceans, to the amazing forests and grasslands, we get to see the unbelievable variety of life that we are all blessed with. I think I have watched these videos at least four or five times. Every time you view the absolutely magical flora and fauna of this fantastic planet, you fill your very soul with the joys of creation. It gives you a deep reverence for the ecosystem and all the creatures and life forms that share in this bounty. You learn to truly respect the interdependence of the countless beings in the natural world. Everything is connected in a mind-blowing web of give and take— the tides, the fungi, the storms, the microorganisms, the polar ice caps. It's an astounding ebb and flow that works with undeniable precision.

Why is it we're not more aware of this life-giving sphere of abundance? Why do we continue to take this wonderland for granted and not give it the love and care that it deserves?

Perhaps, it's because we have considered ourselves separate from its ever-present bosom. Maybe we feel we're above all of this life-sustaining splendor. Whatever the reasons, it's now time for us to open our eyes and give this blue marble its proper recognition.

This planet does not require our existence to continue its evolution. It's actually us who need this place to be healthy and to thrive. We are the ones who benefit from all the fruits that this green jewel provides—the air we breathe, the water that quenches our thirst and the nourishment that fills our stomachs and feeds our families. We are so lucky to be able to enjoy this natural bonanza of treasures.

Let's reignite our passion and connection to the wetlands, to the savannas, to the lakes and streams, to the mountains and valleys. Let's revel in the purity and the sustenance that surrounds us and keeps us alive and happy.

Let's open our hearts to the beauty of life. Let's show Mother Earth we are really thankful for everything she has given us.

CHAPTER 10

ABUNDANCE

Let's consider one of the greatest gifts that we've been given as human beings…our senses. Our abilities to see, hear, smell, taste and touch are without a doubt one of life's true blessings. As I look out my back window now, the signs of spring are emerging. A beautiful red cardinal is preening its feathers in a nearby tree; the daffodils are stretching their brilliant yellow petals towards the sun; a fresh, cool breeze wafts into the room as does the scent of my wife's homemade banana bread. The sounds of migrating songbirds and children playing ring out in the distance. I look forward to the taste of rhubarb and asparagus that I know is just around the corner. I can feel the sun's warm rays caress my skin through the windowpane. Spring is a magical season that is oh so short, but oh so wonderful.

Our senses can conjure up so many memories for us, if we just pay attention. We've all had moments in our lives where a song, a smell, or a taste unlocks a flood of emotions, reminding us how lucky we are to be alive.

Thinking of the powerful impact of sensory pleasures reminds me of the time my wife decided to throw me a surprise party on my 40th birthday. She pulled it off about two weeks before my actual birthday.

I was told there was something that I needed to see but would have to be blindfolded beforehand, so as not to give away the mystery. Nicole carefully led me to the car and made sure I couldn't see a thing. Then she locked the doors, put up the windows and covered my ears so I couldn't hear. As we were driving, she occasionally pulled off the road and did some quick donuts in a parking lot to disorient me even more. I had absolutely no idea where I was or where the hell I was going. I couldn't see or hear. What a strange and unique experience.

Finally, after what seemed like hours, we reached our destination. Nicole gently guided me out of the vehicle, and we slowly walked to the secret location. Now remember, I had no clue where the heck I was at this point, and I had been deprived of both sight and sound. Suddenly, we stopped, and Nicole slowly removed the coverings on both my eyes and ears.

What a flood of awesomeness that moment was! As soon as I could see and hear, the whole scene came rushing in. I instantly recognized that I was back in my hometown (a two-hour drive from where we lived at the time), and all my high school friends were there to celebrate my turning forty.

Wow…it was almost indescribable. Having my senses turned off for a couple of hours and then having everything come blasting back into reality gave an incredible jolt to the brain. Everyone was smiling and laughing and wishing me a happy birthday. It was overwhelming. Not only was I washed over by a wave of sensory stimulation, but I was moved that my lovely wife Nicole and all my old buddies had taken the time to create such a moment. I'll never forget the immense shower of sensations and emotions.

It's moments like these that make me grateful to be alive and to get to experience such vibrations of love. We've all had times in our lives when we have gotten to feel these breezes of affection.

One of the great blessings about being raised in southern Ontario is the bounty of fresh produce grown in the fertile soils of Essex County. There is an incredible abundance of both fruit and vegetables —a true **cornucopia** of just about anything you want. We're talking strawberries, raspberries, peaches, melons and cherries...carrots, tomatoes, sweet corn, peppers and zucchinis. Whatever your heart desires, chances are the local produce stands can provide it.

I was fortunate enough to work on a farm back in the 1980s when I was still in high school. I was able to experience many fascinating aspects of being employed at a multi-crop business. It was both stimulating and physically challenging.

As a teenager, I didn't really appreciate the little things in life. Now that I'm older and wiser, I realize now how amazing that busy little farm actually was. We got to work in the fresh air, feel the sun and the warm breeze coming off the lake, smell the pungent soil and the sweet scent of ripe peaches, taste the sweat and flavor of truly hard labor and touch the fresh foliage of mature fruit trees and grapevines. Every day was different depending on the weather, the produce in season and the amount of work that had to get done. A perk of the job was that we got to eat whatever we were picking. I can't tell you how many strawberries or peaches I got to enjoy in the five summers that I spent in those bountiful fields. It really gets to become part of you…the dirt, the toil, the wind, the humidity, the satisfaction…and knowing that your efforts are going to eventually feed others and fill their stomachs with goodness.

It's early May right now, and the orchards in the fields in the area are coming to life. It always delights me when I get to see the blossoms on the trees, the fresh sprouts bursting from the ground, and the feel of summer fast approaching. What a thrill to know that soon the local fruit stands will be chock-full of delicious offerings. Just thinking about it makes my mouth water and my stomach grumble. It really is a wonderful feeling to be aware of how fortunate we all are to get to enjoy such savory treasures.

There are many places in the world that offer these kinds of pleasures. Locations of abundance and magic that provide us with sustenance and stimulation that we all desire. I was lucky enough to be a small part of this incredible harvest; and, to this day, I am filled with appreciation for the opportunity to stay connected to this place I call home.

I hope everyone can one day experience such gratitude and feel what it's like to be in touch with the earth beneath one's feet and the air that swirls around us and gives us life.

THE POWER TO CHOOSE

We all make choices in life. In fact, we are doing it constantly, every single day.

Some believe these choices are solely based on pleasure or pain. Others feel our decisions are determined by one's mood or circumstances. What influences your decisions?

Are we motivated by something more than just primal instincts or the fickle desires of human nature? Is it possible there is a deeper, more powerful force involved in decision-making?

I believe we are, and it's much more than what we are usually aware of. If we really go deep and look at our underlying reasons for the options we pick, there is one overriding influence. It may not be clear in the moment we make our choice, but this invisible force is always in play.

Can you guess what it is?

It's love! Now this may sound strange if all you are deciding on is what kind of sandwich you want or what movie you feel like watching. But believe me when I say love is the hidden arbiter and final word in everything you choose.

The COVID-19 pandemic has called for many decisions to be made and will require some big choices in the days to come. We may have to follow our moral compass, and not just science, to help guide us in these challenging times.

We've all faced dilemmas in this life and have based our actions on what we felt was right for us at the time. The key to making the wisest call in any circumstances solely lies in our connection to the power of love. The highest choice will always be one that comes from the heart.

Feelings of need and fear will sometimes arise in life, but we do not have to succumb to their influence. All we ever have to do is let our naturally compassionate spirit rule the day.

When the path we are on is steeped in kindness and trust, there is no reason to be afraid. A caring road is always the best way forward in handling any disease, including one that is fraught with suffering and loss.

CHAPTER 12

CHOOSING LOVE, NOT FEAR

T he frontline workers during this crisis are truly amazing people.

Every time they show up for work, they are putting themselves at risk whether they work in a hospital, home, grocery store or any other "essential services" location. They are making a choice every day to put themselves in harm's way.

Now some may say people make this decision based on the fear of losing their job or not having enough money to pay the bills. This is actually not the case. What they're really doing is simply making a choice that is motivated by the heart—either love for themselves or love for others. This is as it should be. When we flavor our decisions with a generous helping of kindness, we are aligning ourselves with the flow of life.

We are seeing nurses and doctors coming out of retirement to lend a hand during the outbreak. Companies are choosing to help out by producing the shields, gloves and other protective gear that care workers require to do their work. We are seeing a flood of compassion and empathy pour out to the places and people that are still vulnerable to the virus.

CHAPTER 13

FEAR

As we press on during this pandemic, we continue our lives as we always have, in the sense that the future is continually unknown to us. Virus or no virus—tomorrow is a never-ending mystery that calls out to our spirits. None of us completely knows what's around the next bend in the road. Whatever is around the corner, we can be sure that putting our trust in love and hope is the best way forward.

Fear is one of life's great illusions. The more we become aware of this understanding, the better we will be able to design and enjoy the days that lay ahead of us. What is fear, anyway? Is it even real?

Usually the things that we are afraid of never actually happen. Most of the scary possibilities that frighten us exist purely in our imagination. The truth is, even though it may feel completely and utterly real, much of what we fear is a mirage.

We possess this emotion because we think it will provide protection from the threats that are trying to take hold and mess up our lives. In reality, most of these supposed terrors are simply holding us back from claiming and living our magnificent adventure.

Did you know that more people are afraid of public speaking than they are of death? Can you believe that? They are absolutely terrified of getting up in front of an audience and doing something as easy as opening their mouth and talking.

In my younger years, I was familiar with the dread and dismay of giving a speech in front of a crowd. My hands would sweat; my knees would knock; and my throat would tighten. The very thought of stepping on stage would fill me with distress and anxiety. My mind and body were scared shitless. What if I messed up? What if they laughed at me? What if I forget what I want to say and completely freeze up?

This kind of fright can be absolutely debilitating, and feelings of horror can utterly consume you. It isn't until you realize that this overwhelming sense of panic and concern is merely a fantasy that you can finally get a grip on your true abilities. Once you awaken to your hidden powers within, you can overcome this illusory trepidation and claim what's rightfully yours.

I am currently a member of an organization called Toastmasters International, where I am able to practice and enjoy the art of public speaking. So far, no one has perished while giving a talk in front of the group members. In fact, as each month goes by, my fellow participants in the club are getting better and more confident with every speech they deliver.

The jitters and angst that accompany most people when they contemplate expressing themselves in front of an audience will easily vanish into the air once they recognize the power of love and courage that they possess. They finally come to understand that this fear was always a figment of their imagination and that life is so much more rewarding and enjoyable when they become aware of their true potential.

CHAPTER 14

INTEGRITY

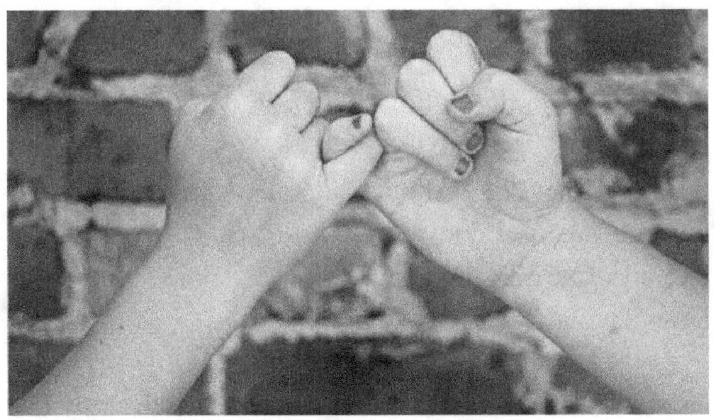

As we move forward in contending with the realities of a post-pandemic world, it is essential that we all work together to create a new way of life. This will require a great amount of effort and a whole new level of integrity. We must rely on everyone to do their part and keep their word. It's going to take each one of us to promise we will do what we say we are going to do.

This new reality will increase the urgency for us to honor our declarations. We must both cultivate our own integrity and grow in trust of others in order to ensure our collective success. This unwritten social contract has always been in play in our daily lives. However, it's going to be even more relevant as we find our way in the days to come.

I think this will hark us back to the days when people made arrangements with each other merely on the seal of a handshake and an agreement to keep their promises. Some people may not realize this, but there was a time when most of our interactions with each other were based on this kind of commitment. My mom would call this "the good old days."

The New World we will live in is going to awaken us to an increased expectation of dependability and respect. We now know how intertwined all our lives are, and we are going to lean on each other to rise to new heights of growth.

When my wife was diagnosed with terminal cancer, we were both taken by surprise and very uncertain as to what our response would be. Nicole would have to get a stem cell transplant, and this would involve a six-month treatment plan and a great deal of sacrifice and discomfort.

We broke the news to my mom, and amazingly she rose to the occasion as only a mother could. She told us that she would help in any way possible. She gave us her word that we were a family and that whatever was necessary to keep Nicole alive would most definitely happen. We decided that we would all live together and focus on Nicole's recovery.

There's no doubt in my mind that if my mom hadn't made this commitment and stood by her promise, my wife would no longer be here. My mom's huge heart and her choice of integrity and love saved Nicole's life. I will forever be grateful for everything that was given to us in our time of distress.

These decisions to be honorable and loving are happening every day. They always have been. It's only now we are realizing how critical it is to keep our commitments.

The pandemic has opened our eyes to the essential connection we have to standing by our words. This newfound understanding will propel us to a better way of living and accelerate the natural evolution of humanity.

CHAPTER 15

ALWAYS KEEP YOUR WORD

When I was living in downtown Windsor, Ontario back in the early 1990s, I used to enjoy talking to some of the characters that hung out at the local street corners.

One of my favorites was an older gentleman named Jack, who was a Jehovah's Witness. He would set up on the busiest intersections in the whole city and share his Bible lessons with anyone who was interested. I used to spend a few hours with him every time I had the chance, because it was very stimulating to ask him questions about life and listen to his interactions with other curious pedestrians. He was always kind and extremely patient with whoever came his way. I deeply admired him for his confidence and conviction. He was truly committed to his faith, and at times he was confronted and challenged by people who did not share his point of view.

I'll never forget one exchange when he was in conversation with a very devout Catholic. They disagreed about what happens when we die, and the debate got quite heated. The Catholic guy got upset about Jack's position on the afterlife and felt so irritated that he turned beet red. Ranting and raving, he told Jack that he hoped he would burn in hell for his blasphemous beliefs. Jack never flinched. He simply smiled, wished him well and waved to the man as he jumped onto one of the city buses, still screaming at the top of his lungs. I was a bit shocked by this whole episode, but I definitely respected Jack's calm demeanor and ability to remain so steady throughout the entire encounter.

Jack had a powerful dedication to his faith, and he kept his word to his God no matter the circumstances. Such devotion and integrity can sometimes be hard to find in this uncertain world. Being around someone who is completely reliable and committed to their promises is a wonderful thing to behold.

I didn't always agree with Jack's point of view, nor did I share his faith in a Judeo-Christian deity. Sometimes we would just agree to disagree and wish each other the best in life and whatever was to come in the future.

I will always remember him and those interesting moments on the street corner—a man who kept his word, no matter what life decided to throw his way. Good for you, my old friend!

CHAPTER 16

THE SANCTITY OF LIFE

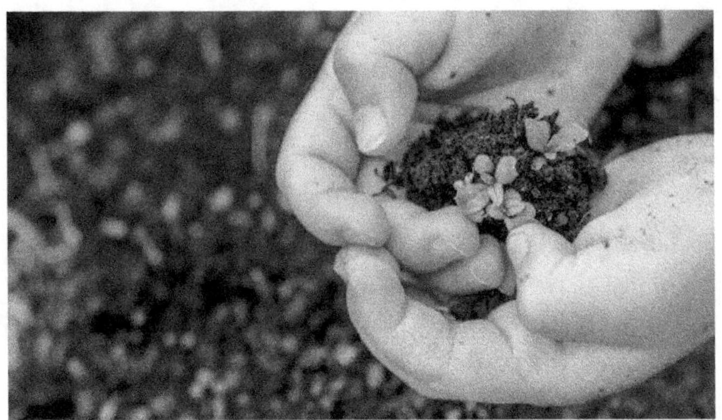

As I continue to express my thoughts and feelings, I gaze out in my backyard and see the signs of spring blooming to life. A fresh, cool breeze drifts into the room, and a faint scent of magnolia perfumes the air that I breathe. A bright yellow goldfinch perches on a nearby maple tree, and the distinct sounds of nature are coming alive all around me. What an absolute rush of pure delight and sensory pleasure it is to behold the coming of my favorite season.

Now of course the virus really doesn't care about what season it is, or what can be felt and enjoyed at this moment in our time. But I can't help but notice the magic that is unfolding outside my window.

What a blessing it is to witness the sanctity of life. We are continually surrounded and embraced by the wonders of creation. It is evident, now more than ever, that human beings are but a part of a much larger and grander web of existence.

While we are somewhat at the mercy of COVID-19, we can rise above this by recognizing that life will continue; and we must now expand our approach to interacting with the planet. It is readily apparent that we are vulnerable to the vibrations of the natural world. It would be wise to understand our place in this relationship. This awesome planet is our one and only home, and it is time for us to completely open our hearts to this treasure we've been given.

There are people and cultures in this world that have known this for eons, and their reverence for the earth has remained an integral part of their soul. Respect for all life is where we are ultimately headed.

Now is the time for us to make the next leap in our evolution. Today is our moment to follow the wisdom of the ancients. All in this world is sacred.

Let's trust in this knowledge and take that next critical step. Homo sapiens are ready for what comes next.

CHAPTER 17

LIFE AND DEATH

I want to pose a question. Now get ready because it's definitely a doozy. In fact, it's probably one of the biggest, most important and profound questions that you can ask yourself—a mystery that has been wrestled with for millennia. Are you ready for it?

What do you believe is going to happen to you when you die?

Do you believe there is an afterlife awaiting your arrival?

Are you looking forward to being "in heaven" when you pass on?

Seeing some of your family and friends?

Or, do you think that this life is all there is; and once it's over, we're all just dust in the wind?

Now, why is it absolutely essential that we ask ourselves these most powerful questions? Because, it can provide us with a deep, revealing understanding of who we truly are and why we're really here. It gets us to become much more aware of the significance of our daily choices in life and helps us to open our eyes to what is of the utmost value to us.

Think about it:

Is what you believe about death reflected in how you live your life?

If you believe in an immortal soul, is that an integral guide to your personal choices?

Whatever we believe about our ultimate destiny has a powerful effect on our experience of being human.

Dig deep. Go into yourself and ask one of the definitive questions of all ages:

What will happen to me when I die?

CHAPTER 18

WISDOM: DO WHAT WORKS

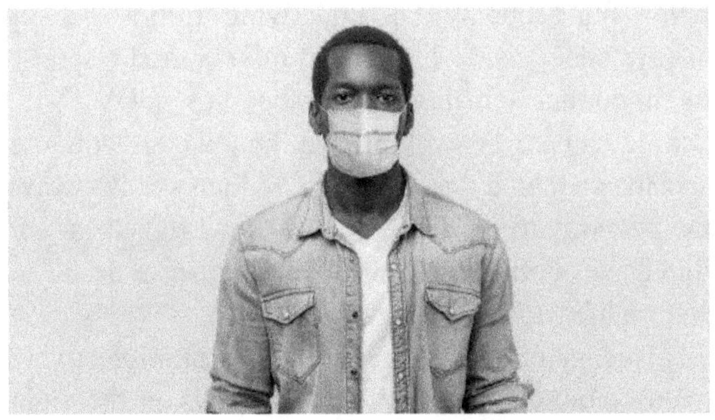

One of the things that really stands out to me during this health crisis is the emphasis of the medical community on "getting it right the first time." There's a general consensus by most infectious disease specialists that it is essential that we do everything properly: social distancing, quarantining, wearing coverings for your nose and mouth, and of course plenty of handwashing.

These practices present what are believed to be best practices—the most effective means of preventing the virus from spreading. Most people seem to feel that these behaviors represent a reasonable and appropriate response. It seems to make sense that we would listen to the experts and follow their advice regarding what is the wisest way to handle this pandemic.

There is a greater lesson to be learned regarding how to deal with this virus and how to eventually revive our economy. The underlying truth is that it's always beneficial to have a carefully crafted response to important situations. Whether it's COVID-19, getting us back to work or even how we are going to socialize again, a wisely considered answer is always the best way to go. This is not the time to be hasty or impulsive, even though most of us share a desire to restore life back to the way it was.

This is our chance to intelligently and selectively make some choices that will move us in the right direction, on a new path that can take us to a higher way of living.

It reminds me of a show I used to love to watch, *Star Trek: The Next Generation*. Whenever the crew of the *USS Enterprise* got themselves into a predicament, they were usually very measured and deliberate in how they handled different situations. There was an informed and nuanced response to whatever challenges came their way. They were focussed on using their intellect and wisdom to come up with the best solutions. Yes, they had advanced technology, and yes, they had access to artificial intelligence. However, they still relied on their instincts and intuition. They took a highly evolved road to finding the answers.

This is how we should move forward in dealing with the difficulties of a viral attack. It's going to be up to us to figure out the smartest way to minimize the distress and maximize the success.

We can elevate our world to greater heights if we can effectively use our collective knowledge to our advantage. This is going to be key...a civilized and ultimately loving answer that everyone can understand and accept.

CHAPTER 19

LIFE IS A RISK

Throughout these unusual times, we often hear people say to each other, "Stay safe" or "Be safe." Love and good intentions drive these sentiments, and it's always nice to hear someone wishing us safety and good vibrations.

However, the truth is, life is a risky endeavor.

Even before the pandemic arrived, being human has been fraught with pitfalls. Every time we open our eyes and get out of bed, we enter the world that will continually throw hazards and challenges our way. Since the beginning of our history, we have been navigating and coping with a multitude of risks. Whether it has been saber-tooth tigers, natural disasters, diseases, pestilence, car crashes, or pollution

—we are constantly dealing with life's slings and arrows.

The COVID-19 virus is our latest reminder that being alive entails navigating a minefield of dangers. We all want to feel secure and appreciate the concern others show us in times of calamity. It's instinctual for parents to protect their children, and it has benefited us immensely to look out for one another whenever the next black cat crosses our path. At the same time, it's important for us to recognize that every day we spend on this earth will be filled with possible pain and suffering.

People don't think twice when they jump in their car or boat, when they go for a run or ride their bike, when they step on a ladder or onto a roof. Heck, even climbing a set of stairs can lead to disaster. There is affliction and death every day on this planet, and none of us really know how much time we have. We are fragile creatures, and even though we can't live our lives in a state of paranoia, it does serve us to be aware that this world is filled with hornet nests. Does this mean we should throw the covers over our heads and never take a chance on anything? Of course not. But it does invite us to be much more cognizant of what life may have in store for us.

Sometimes tumult and turmoil provide valuable lessons and give us deeper appreciation and understanding of what is really of significance. When you taste the bitterness of disappointment and despair, it can make your triumphs and successes that much sweeter.

There's nothing inherently wrong with taking chances. Crossing the road involves rolling the dice, whether we realize it or not. There's little reason to be afraid of traffic, bees, spiders, ghosts, heights, or even viruses so long as we remain aware that these things have always been a part of life, in one way or another. In fact, it makes our existence that much more rewarding if we remain grounded in the reality that we are only here for a finite amount of time, and that it's up to us to savor the moments.

This viral outbreak is our clarion call to remember why we are here and the brief and precious nature of the dance of life.

So, don't be terrified or distraught over what is happening in our world right now. Just simply open your eyes to the veracity of it all.

We're here for a good time, not a long time. That's what makes it so special.

CHAPTER 20

RETURN TO OUR ROOTS

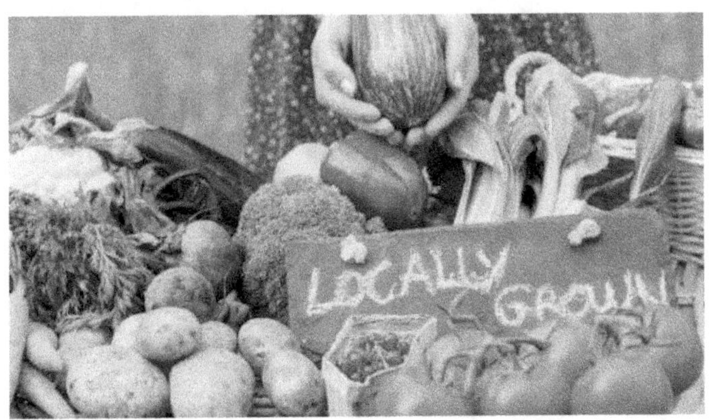

The realities and consequences of the COVID-19 virus have made it quite clear that perhaps it's been a tad unwise for us to depend on essential goods that are manufactured on the other side of the planet.

Having our medical supplies and pharmaceuticals made halfway around the world from us doesn't really make a lot of sense if we need those items right away. We were already realizing this folly with our food supply, even before the pandemic arrived.

In North America, there is a movement towards farm to table production, and there is a growing demand for sourcing our agricultural food stuffs from local farmers. People are increasingly wanting to know where their meat, dairy and fruits and vegetables come from. We're rediscovering what we once knew and practiced—that it's much wiser for us to produce our daily bread close to home. This new type of "enlightened" consumption is merely returning to the ways of our forefathers.

Our ancestors grew up in a time where most of what they purchased was made very near to where they lived, or at least it was created in their own country. They had a much better understanding and connection to where their goods were coming from. This viral episode reminds us that it's important to be aware of where stuff comes from, and it's essential that we insist that more of what we consume should be produced closer to our backyards.

This is in direct harmony with the whole concept of "think globally, act locally." We can act in a local way, and at the same time realize that this has a global impact. We can focus our energy on rebuilding nearby economies and reconnecting to the roots of our past.

Whether it's food coming from farms a few kilometers away, beer from your hometown brewery, technology from an innovative start-up just down the street, or even attending a performance at your local theater, we can all benefit from the reprised relationship with our origins.

Don't be surprised if you see even more of a desire for old-school merchants who know their customers' names and go the extra mile. This is how it used to be—people taking care of each other and having a mutually appreciated connection.

Welcome to the New World. It's not so much different in some ways as the old one.

CHAPTER 21

THE PURITY OF GIVING

If we carefully examine what we're all going through right now, it becomes obvious that the main thrust and solution is to address the current viral situation. The only answer that will ultimately suffice in this crazy ordeal is for us to open our hearts and love each other like we've never done before.

It's going to require a whole new level of compassion and empathy. When we look out into the world and see the suffering and pain that people are experiencing, it is essential that we stay aware that it is <u>all</u> of us who are struggling…it is <u>all</u> of us that desire comfort and connection…it is <u>all</u> of us that will benefit from an all-encompassing gesture of love and kindness.

We are on the precipice of a new way of being. It's time for us to make the jump into the great unknown and find a deeper, more powerful method of caring for one another. This is the next natural step in our growth as a species. It is love that will get us through this, and it's our capacity to see the universe through others' eyes that will carry us to the other side of this challenge.

All we have to do is watch the daily news to see countless examples of people looking out for each other and finding ways to show that they truly want to be of service.

I just saw a story yesterday about a 100-year-old gentleman who was walking laps in an attempt to raise money for a fund that would support those who are in need of food and essential supplies. So far, he has raised somewhere around fifty-three million dollars. Wow, what an incredible example of the power of the human spirit. If this elderly man can reach down deep and find the strength to do something for his fellow human beings, just imagine what is possible if we all were to commit ourselves to discovering different ways to touch each other's lives.

It doesn't have to be a grand gesture. It could be as simple as checking in on our neighbors or making a small donation to a local food bank or charity. Simple efforts can amount to a mountain of assistance, if we find that wonderful place inside of us that is eager to make itself known. No expression of love is too small, and no attempt at kindness is insignificant. It all adds up to a treasure trove of memories and connections.

We are wired for this kind of unconditional affection. We were born for this moment where we can all make a substantial impact on each other's well-being and future. This really is our time to shine. It is imperative that we grab onto this moment and take our world to new heights of existence. If even a small child can muster up the courage and conviction to help humanity, then surely every single one of us can discover our path to sincerity and love.

Do you believe there is such a thing as unconditional love? Have you ever experienced it before, whether as the giver or the recipient? Do we even know what this concept actually means?

In this very moment, the examples I can think of and truly relate to are the love I have felt and witnessed from my mother, and perhaps the affection, attention and devotion I have seen from dogs. In both cases, I have been on the receiving end of this most amazing and special kind of emotion. Since I have never known the feeling of having my own children, I can't honestly say I have ever felt this expression of complete and utter no-strings-attached loyalty. To embody such an all-encompassing commitment has to be the ultimate example of how deep the river of love actually flows. Its depth knows no limits and to experience such a feeling must be at times both heartbreaking and absolutely indescribable.

As we emerge from this crazy pandemic and face the challenges that will inevitably come our way, it is going to require a whole new level of love for humanity in order for us to ensure our success. It's going to take an expansion of our hearts like we've never known before as human beings. We will have to explore the depths of our souls and reach out to one another as a mother does for her child. Now, why do I say this?

It's because I believe that the realities of living in a post-COVID-19 world are going to test us to the very core of our being. We will be faced with unprecedented situations that will demand an incredible amount of financial, emotional, moral and spiritual conviction.

Are we going to build a new holistic approach to living, or are we simply just going to go back to being asleep at the wheel?

The truth that lives in the demands of this new reality are commanding us as a species to rise up and become more empathetic and compassionate than ever before.

The future is NOW.

We must answer the call of universal LOVE.

We are faced with our greatest opportunity.

Will we respond with a quality of devotion and sacrifice that only a mother knows?

Only time will tell.

ABOUT CHRIS FORMAN

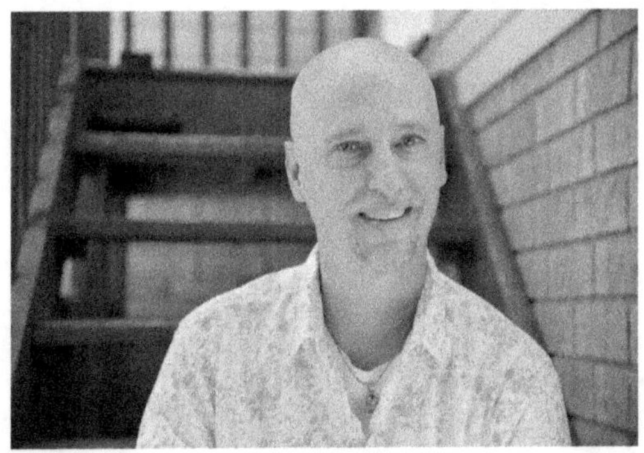

Chris Forman is a transformational speaker and author who inspires his audiences to awaken as individuals and members of the human family.

Chris is the Founder & CEO of Personal Sage, and the creator of the forthcoming video series, *True Wealth: A 30-Day Adventure to Discover Your Inner Riches*. Through his Personal Sage Coaching, he provides 1:1 inspiration and insight to ALL who are ready to take the next step on their journey to transformation.

A professional bartender for over twenty-five years, Chris has gleaned uncommon wisdom from conversations with thousands of diverse patrons, leading to deep insights into the human condition.

He lives in Leamington, Ontario, Canada, with his beloved bride, Nicole.

LET'S STAY CONNECTED

Thanks so much for reading *A New Way To Live*.

I have lots of exciting plans and projects in store for the coming months, including the release of my next book, *True Wealth*.

Let's connect so you can stay in the loop, and I can support you on YOUR journey as well!

✉ chris@personal-sage.com

🌐 personal-sage.com

📷 @personal_sage

f fb.com/personalsage

 **Don't miss a thing!**

Sign-up for my newsletter at personal-sage.com and you'll get the **latest developments** here at *Personal Sage*, including **exclusive access** to **special offers**.

A Free Gift for You!

As a thank you for purchasing this book, I'd like to offer you a FREE audio download of my keynote presentation, based on the content in my forthcoming book, *True Wealth*.

To claim your free gift, go to:

personal-sage.com/gift

COMING SOON...

9 781777 310349